Eco-crafts

40 FUN EARTH-FRIENDLY PROJECTS

written by
Marcy Morin
and **Heidi E. Thompson**

CAPSTONE PRESS
a capstone imprint

Published by Capstone Press, an imprint of Capstone.
1710 Roe Crest Drive, North Mankato, Minnesota 56003
capstonepub.com

Library of Congress Cataloging-in-Publication Data
Names: Morin, Marcy, 1980- author. | Thompson, Heidi E., author.
Title: Eco-crafts : 40 fun earth-friendly projects / by Marcy Morin and Heidi E. Thompson.
Description: North Mankato, Minnesota : Capstone Press, [2022] | Series: Eco crafts | Includes bibliographical references. | Audience: Ages 8-11| Audience: Grades 4-6 | Summary: "Wait! Don't toss that milk jug or cardboard cup into the recycling bin yet! And hang on to those old jeans, shrunken sweaters, and stained T-shirts. Give cardboard, paper, plastic, and clothing completely new uses as you make one-of-a-kind eco-creations with 40 fun ideas. A pet bed, party piñata, suncatcher, and more crafts are just a snip, fold, or stitch away!"-- Provided by publisher.
Identifiers: LCCN 2021029707 | ISBN 9781666348026 (paperback) | ISBN 9781666348033 (pdf)
Subjects: LCSH: Handicraft for children--Juvenile literature. | Waste paper--Recycling--Juvenile literature. | Plastics--Recycling--Juvenile literature. | Textile fabrics--Recycling--Juvenile literature.
Classification: LCC TT160 .M637 2022 | DDC 745.5083--dc23
LC record available at https://lccn.loc.gov/2021029707

Credits
Designer: Bobbie Nuytten

All internet sites appearing in back matter were available and accurate when this book was sent to press.

For my Mama, for teaching me all things crafty!
—MM

For Bray, Cole, and Isaac, who keep me creative and on my toes. —HT

Printed and bound in China. 4545

TABLE OF CONTENTS

Paper can be used for a lot more than writing! Maybe you'll craft a **suncatcher** out of used tissue paper or an **envelope** out of an old map. You might even make a **bouquet of flowers** out of yesterday's newspaper!

Rather than donating your old clothes, you can upcycle them instead! Maybe you'll craft a **scrunchie** out of an old shirt or a **beanie** out of a worn sweater. An old towel can even become a monster **laundry hamper**!

You can use plastic for so many crafts! Maybe you'll make a **bird feeder** out of a takeout container or an **outdoor pillow** stuffed with used shopping bags. You can even turn old plastic toys into **stylish decor**!

All types of cardboard can be used for crafting! Maybe you'll make a **colorful piñata**. You could create a cool **cell phone holder**. You may even build a cardboard **bee sanctuary** to hang from a tree!

GOOD DAY

CREATE WITH CARDBOARD

CARDBOARD IS EVERYWHERE!

Many everyday items come packaged in it, from cereal to shoes. When we're done with cardboard, we recycle it. But with creativity, you can turn used cardboard into new items!

The crafts in this book use materials you'll likely find at home. Is there something you can't find? Think of ways to adapt the project using items you do have.

BE SURE TO ASK FOR AN ADULT'S HELP WITH ANY SHARP TOOLS OR OBJECTS.

WITH CARDBOARD, THERE'S NO LIMIT TO WHAT YOU CAN CREATE.

PARTY PIÑATA MONSTER

WHAT'S BETTER THAN A PARTY? A PARTY **WITH A PIÑATA!** TRANSFORM AN EMPTY TISSUE BOX INTO A CANDY CONTAINER. THEN FIND A BAT AND HAVE A BLAST!

WHAT YOU NEED

- ribbon
- ruler
- scissors
- pencil
- empty tissue box
- crepe paper
- craft glue
- foam brush
- candy
- googly eyes or paper and markers

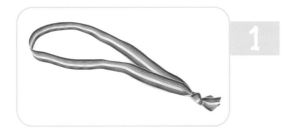

1 Cut a 24-inch (61-centimeter) piece of ribbon. Fold it in half. Then knot the loose ends.

2 Use the pencil to poke a small hole in a top corner of the box. Thread the ribbon's loop through the poked hole from inside the box.

ECO FACTS Facial tissues are made from paper pulp. Americans wipe their noses with billions of disposable tissues every year.

3   Cut a long strip of crepe paper. Fold the strip on top of itself into small sections. Make each about 4 inches (10 cm) wide.

4   Cut small slits halfway up the folded crepe paper. Unfold the strip.

5   Brush a line of glue around the sides of the box, starting at the bottom. Wrap the strip of crepe paper around the box.

6   Repeat steps 3 through 5 to cover the sides of the box. Then cover the bottom of the box with layers of more cut crepe paper.

7   Fill the box with candy through its top opening. Then cover the top of the box with more cut crepe paper.

• FINAL STEP!

GLUE EYES ON YOUR PIÑATA TO MAKE IT A GOOFY MONSTER!

MOSAIC PET PORTRAIT

LOOKING FOR A PET PROJECT? THIS CRAFT IS A GEOMETRIC WORK OF ART. MAKE A MOSAIC MASTERPIECE OF YOUR FAVORITE ANIMAL!

WHAT YOU NEED

- paperboard (cereal or cracker boxes)
- scissors
- pencil
- paint and paintbrush
- craft glue
- corrugated cardboard box

1

Cut one large side from the paperboard to make a flat sheet. Draw the outline of your favorite pet on the sheet.

2

Cut out the shape.

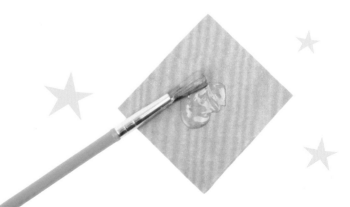

3 Paint the shape one color.

4 Cut shapes from extra paperboard to create your animal's features. This could include ears, eyes, a nose or beak, or scales. Paint the shapes other colors and glue them to your pet cutout.

5 Ask an adult to cut a square of the corrugated cardboard. This will be a mount for your pet mosaic. Paint the cardboard and let it dry.

FINAL STEP!

GLUE YOUR PET PORTRAIT TO THE CARDBOARD AND DISPLAY IT!!

DESKTOP ORGANIZER

DO YOU HAVE A MESSY DESK? MAKE A STACKABLE ORGANIZER OUT OF A FEW SUPPLIES. THIS CRAFT WILL HELP UNCLUTTER YOUR DESK. AND IT'LL KEEP CARDBOARD CLUTTER FROM ENDING UP IN A LANDFILL!

WHAT YOU NEED

- shoebox
- scissors
- pencil
- ruler
- craft knife
- colorful duct tape
- hot glue and hot glue gun

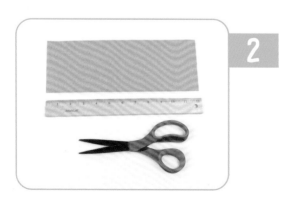

1 Open the shoebox up at its seams. Cut along the folds to make several cardboard pieces.

2 Measure and cut a 12-by-4-inch (30.5-by-10-cm) strip.

12

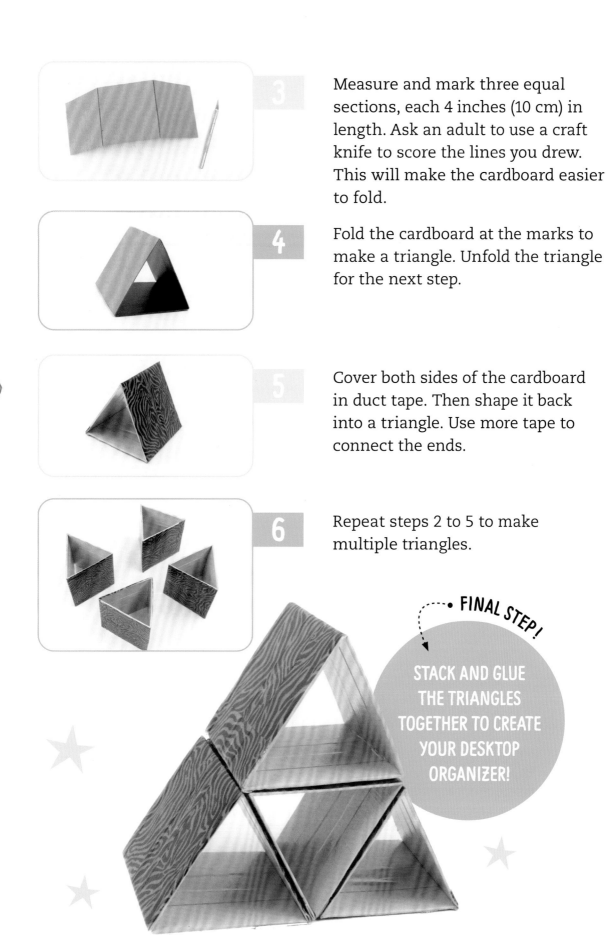

3 Measure and mark three equal sections, each 4 inches (10 cm) in length. Ask an adult to use a craft knife to score the lines you drew. This will make the cardboard easier to fold.

4 Fold the cardboard at the marks to make a triangle. Unfold the triangle for the next step.

5 Cover both sides of the cardboard in duct tape. Then shape it back into a triangle. Use more tape to connect the ends.

6 Repeat steps 2 to 5 to make multiple triangles.

• FINAL STEP!

STACK AND GLUE THE TRIANGLES TOGETHER TO CREATE YOUR DESKTOP ORGANIZER!

LEAF ORNAMENTS

RE-CREATE NATURE'S BEAUTY INDOORS! REPURPOSE PAPERBOARD AND MAGAZINE PAGES TO MAKE **COLORFUL LEAVES.** THEN HANG THEM IN YOUR HOME.

WHAT YOU NEED

- magazine pages
- hole punch
- pencil
- paperboard (cereal or cracker boxes)
- scissors
- craft glue
- paintbrush
- pushpin
- string

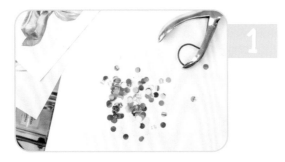

1 Use the hole punch to create piles of confetti out of magazine pages.

2 Cut along the paperboard box seams to create a flat sheet. Draw leaf shapes on the sheet. Cut out the shapes. Draw veins on the leaves if you like. These will peek through the confetti.

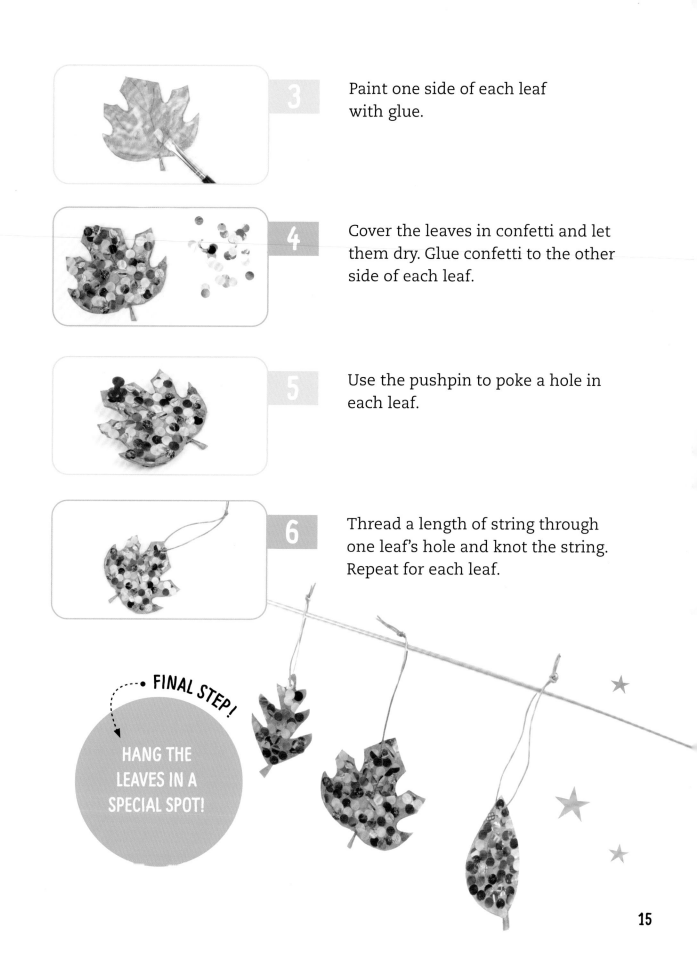

3 Paint one side of each leaf with glue.

4 Cover the leaves in confetti and let them dry. Glue confetti to the other side of each leaf.

5 Use the pushpin to poke a hole in each leaf.

6 Thread a length of string through one leaf's hole and knot the string. Repeat for each leaf.

FINAL STEP!

HANG THE LEAVES IN A SPECIAL SPOT!

✱ BEE ✱ SANCTUARY

BEES ARE NATURE'S GARDENERS. THEY POLLINATE DIFFERENT PLANTS, HELPING TO FORM FRUITS, VEGETABLES, AND EVEN NEW SEEDS. WITHOUT BEES, WE WOULD BE WITHOUT MANY FOODS! REUSE EVERYDAY ITEMS TO CREATE A SAFE PLACE FOR BEES TO NEST.

WHAT YOU NEED

- tall, narrow cardboard box (or paperboard milk carton)
- scissors
- paint and paintbrushes
- clear packing tape
- pencil
- twine
- cardboard tubes
- paper straws
- sticks and twigs

1 Remove the lid or cut the top flaps off the box. Paint the box and let it dry.

2 Wrap clear packing tape around the outside of the box. This will help protect it from rain.

ECO FACTS

Your bee sanctuary will attract cavity-nesting bees. This type of wild bee lays eggs in plant stems and holes in wood. These bees are great pollinators for your garden!

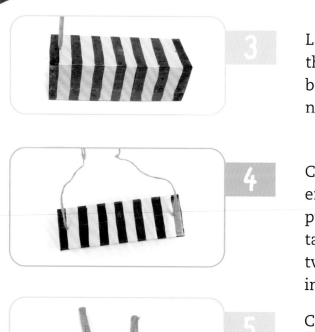

3 Lay the box on one long side. Use the pencil to punch a hole near the box's open end. Punch another hole near its closed end.

4 Cut a piece of twine. Make it long enough to thread through the punched holes and create two long tails outside the box. Thread the twine through the holes from inside the box.

5 Cut a cardboard tube in half the long way. Roll up each half the long way to create two long, thin cylinders. Tape each cylinder together to secure. Repeat this step to make several more cylinders.

6 Trim the cylinders, paper straws, and sticks. Make them a little shorter than the length of the box.

7 Pack the box tightly with the straws, sticks, and cylinders.

• FINAL STEP!

TIE YOUR BEE SANCTUARY SNUGLY TO A TREE BRANCH FACING SOUTH OR SOUTHEAST.

17

PAPERBOARD PLANETS

TURN YOUR EMPTY CEREAL BOXES INTO SPACE ART! COLORFUL STRIPS TRANSFORM INTO SPINNING PLANETS IN THIS FUN CRAFT.

WHAT YOU NEED

- paperboard (cereal or cracker boxes)
- scissors
- paint and paintbrush
- ruler
- pencil
- pushpin
- brads (metal fasteners)
- oil pastels
- yarn

1 Unfold a cereal box. Cut off the flaps. Then cut along one seam. This creates a large, flat sheet of paperboard.

2 Paint each side of the paperboard a different color. Let it dry.

ECO FACTS

A cereal box can be recycled and turned into a new cereal box up to six times. After that, the cardboard's fiber becomes too weak to reuse.

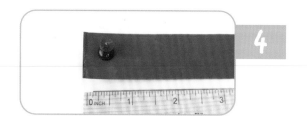

3 Across the paperboard's length, measure and cut out strips that are 1 inch (2.5 cm) wide.

4 Use the pushpin to make a hole about ½ inch (1.3 cm) from each end of each strip. Widen the holes slightly using the tip of the pencil.

5 Stack the strips. Push a brad through their holes on one end. Open the brad to secure it. Secure the other ends of the strips with another brad.

6 Slowly spread the strips out to create a sphere. Decorate the outside of your orb! Use oil pastels to make planetary swirls, rings, and more.

7 Thread a piece of yarn through the top of the sphere. Tie the ends in a knot to make a hanger.

• FINAL STEP!

TRY MAKING MORE SPHERES USING DIFFERENT NUMBERS AND LENGTHS OF STRIPS!

19

WHALE PHONE HOLDER

DOES YOUR PHONE NEED A NICE PLACE TO REST OVERNIGHT? CRAFT A COLORFUL VESSEL TO KEEP IT SAFE ON THE SEAS (OR JUST YOUR NIGHTSTAND). CARDBOARD BECOMES A CUTE WHALE IN A FEW EASY STEPS.

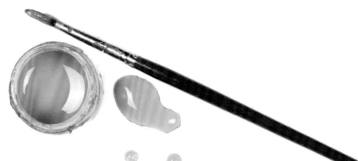

WHAT YOU NEED

- pencil
- corrugated cardboard
- utility knife or scissors
- ruler
- hot glue and hot glue gun
- paint and paintbrush
- markers or gems

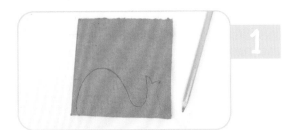

1 Sketch a whale on cardboard. Make the whale about the size of your cell phone.

2 Have an adult cut out your whale shape.

20

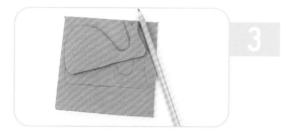

Trace the cutout on another cardboard square. Then have an adult cut out the traced shape as well.

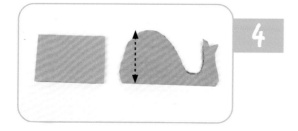

Measure the height of the whale's head. Have an adult cut out a cardboard rectangle that is the whale's height by 3 inches (8 cm). This will be the first connecting piece.

Measure the height of the whale's tail. Have an adult cut out a cardboard rectangle that is the tail's height by 3 inches (8 cm). This is the second connecting piece.

Glue the connecting pieces to your whale so the 3-inch sides are horizontal. This creates the space where your phone will rest.

FINAL STEP!

PAINT THE WHALE AND DECORATE IT USING MARKERS OR GEMS!

GOAT PUPPET

DO YOU HAVE USED CARDBOARD TUBES IN YOUR HOUSE? SAVE THEM FROM THE RECYCLING BIN AND BUILD A PRANCING PUPPET. ONCE YOU HAVE ONE DONE, MAKE MORE ANIMALS!

WHAT YOU NEED

- 2 cardboard tubes
- scissors
- paint and paintbrush
- 2 craft sticks
- string
- pushpin
- toothpick
- ruler
- marker
- pipe cleaner (chenille stem)
- tape

1

Leave one tube whole for your goat's body. Cut off one-third of the other tube. The larger piece of that will be your goat's head.

2

Paint all three tube pieces inside and out. Let them dry.

3

Make an X with the craft sticks. Wrap a piece of string around the point where the sticks cross. Tie the string to secure the sticks.

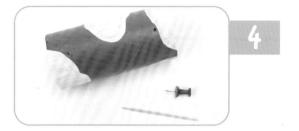

4

Use the pushpin to poke two parallel holes into the body tube. Make one hole at each end along the top of the body. Slightly widen the holes with a toothpick.

5

At one end of the head tube, poke a hole ½ inch (1.3 cm) from the end. Poke a second hole across from the first on the same end of the tube. Make the second hole 1 inch (2.5 cm) in from the end.

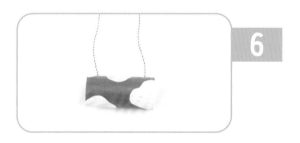

6

Cut two 12-inch (30.5-cm) pieces of string. Tie a knot at one end of each. Then, from inside the tube, thread each unknotted end through one hole in the body tube.

7

In one string, tie a knot where you want the head to rest. Then thread the unknotted end of that string up through the holes in the head tube. Start with the hole that is farther in from the end of the head tube.

Project continued on the next page

8 Grab the X from step 3. Tie the end of each string to opposite ends of the same craft stick.

9 Cut out horns from the remaining cardboard tube. Glue the horns to the head.

10 Draw eyes with the marker.

11 Cut the pipe cleaner into five equal pieces. Use the pushpin to poke four small holes for legs. Make these holes in the underside of the body tube.

ECO FACTS

Shigeru Ban is a Japanese architect. He constructs temporary homes and other buildings out of cardboard tubes. Ban often builds these structures to shelter people whose homes get damaged by natural disasters.

12 Insert a pipe cleaner piece into each leg hole. Bend the pieces inside the tube to secure them in place. Bend the other ends to look like feet.

13 Tape the remaining pipe cleaner piece inside the tube as a tail.

• FINAL STEP!

HOLD AND MOVE THE CRAFT STICK X TO MAKE YOUR PUPPET MOVE. WATCH IT PRANCE, WALK, AND CLIMB!

CARDBOARD CACTUS

PLANTS BRING LIFE TO ANY ROOM! BUT PLANTS ALSO REQUIRE CARE. IF YOU HAVE A HARD TIME REMEMBERING TO WATER, THIS PAPER PLANT IS PERFECT. BUILD IT AND ADMIRE IT. NO CARE NEEDED!

WHAT YOU NEED

- empty oatmeal container or other cylindrical cardboard container
- utility knife
- craft glue
- old magazine
- scissors
- markers
- stickers
- corrugated cardboard
- pencil
- paint and paintbrush
- toothpicks
- hot glue and hot glue gun
- rocks, pebbles, acorns, or other natural materials

1 Ask an adult to cut the container's height to 4 or 5 inches (10 or 13 cm). This will be your planter pot. Use craft glue to decorate it with old magazine page cutouts. Let the glue dry. Then decorate the pot with markers and stickers.

2 Draw two cactus shapes on the corrugated cardboard. Make sure the cactuses can fit inside the container from step 1. Have an adult help you cut out the shapes.

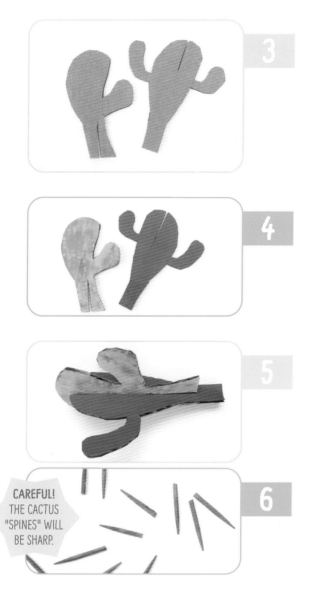

3 Starting from the base, have an adult cut a slit about one-third up the length of one cactus stem. Repeat for the second cactus, but this time cut down starting from the top.

4 Paint the front and back of each cactus and let them dry.

5 Wedge the two cactus pieces together at the slits you created in step 3.

CAREFUL! THE CACTUS "SPINES" WILL BE SHARP.

6 Paint the toothpicks and let them dry. Then cut them into smaller pieces and hot glue these to the cactus as spines.

• FINAL STEP!

PLACE YOUR FINISHED CACTUS IN YOUR DECORATED CONTAINER. FILL AROUND THE CACTUS WITH ROCKS, ACORNS, OR OTHER NATURE ITEMS TO HOLD IT IN PLACE!

MOUNTAIN WALL ART

NATURE SHOWS OFF AWESOME LANDSCAPES DAY AND NIGHT! RE-CREATE A **SCENIC VIEW** WITH SOME CARDBOARD. IF YOU'D LIKE, HIDE TINY LIGHTS IN IT TO MAKE YOUR ARTWORK GLOW!

WHAT YOU NEED

- corrugated cardboard box
- utility knife or scissors
- ruler
- pencil
- paint and paintbrush
- hot glue and hot glue gun
- string of battery-powered LED lights (optional)

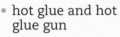

Ask an adult to help you cut three cardboard rectangles. Make the first 12 by 8 inches (30.5 by 20 cm), the second 12 by 6 inches (30.5 by 15 cm), and the third 12 by 3 inches (30.5 by 8 cm).

Draw mountain peaks across the length of the two smaller rectangles. Then cut along the mountaintops.

3 Paint the mountain pieces and the rectangular backboard. Add a moon and stars. Let the paint dry.

4 Have an adult cut out 12 cardboard squares. Make six of the squares 2-by-2-inches (5-by-5-cm). Make the other six squares 1-by-1-inch (2.5-by-2.5-cm).

5 Glue the smaller squares together in three pairs. Repeat with the larger squares.

Project continued on the next page

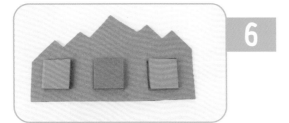

6 Glue the three larger square pairs to the back of the larger mountain piece.

7 Glue the three smaller square pairs to the back of the smaller mountain piece.

8 Line up the bottom of the larger mountain piece with the bottom of the backboard. Glue the mounted square pieces to the backboard.

9 Line up the bottom of the smaller mountain piece with the bottom of the larger mountain piece. Glue its mounted squares on top of the first set of mountains.

ECO FACTS

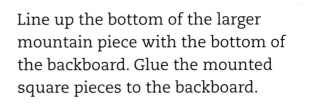
In the United States, more than 90 percent of shipped products are contained in corrugated boxes. This equals more than 80 billion cardboard boxes used each year!

• FINAL STEP!

HANG YOUR WALL ART. IF YOU'D LIKE, TUCK A STRING OF LED LIGHTS BEHIND THE MOUNTAINS TO ADD A STARRY GLOW!

CLOTHING IS EVERYWHERE!

Do you have clothes that you no longer wear? Maybe it's a sweater that's too small or jeans with too many holes. You might also have forgotten towels in the back of a closet. When we're done using these items, we usually donate them. But why not turn old fabric and clothing into useful new items?

CLEAN OUT YOUR CLOSETS, GRAB SOME SCISSORS AND GLUE, AND GET READY TO CRAFT!

DENIM FEATHERS

GRAB A PAIR OF JEANS YOU'VE OUTGROWN AND MAKE SOME DENIM FEATHERS! USE THEM AS BOOKMARKS OR COOL DECOR.

WHAT YOU NEED

- old jeans or jean shorts
- marker
- scissors
- paint and paintbrush (optional)
- yarn
- bead
- toothpick
- hot glue and hot glue gun

1 Lay the jeans on a flat work surface. Find a seam. Draw a simple feather shape with the seam running down the middle.

2 Cut out your feather shape. Make additional cuts from the edge of the feather in toward the seam to create fringe.

ECO FACTS The average American throws away about 80 pounds (36 kilograms) of clothing every year.

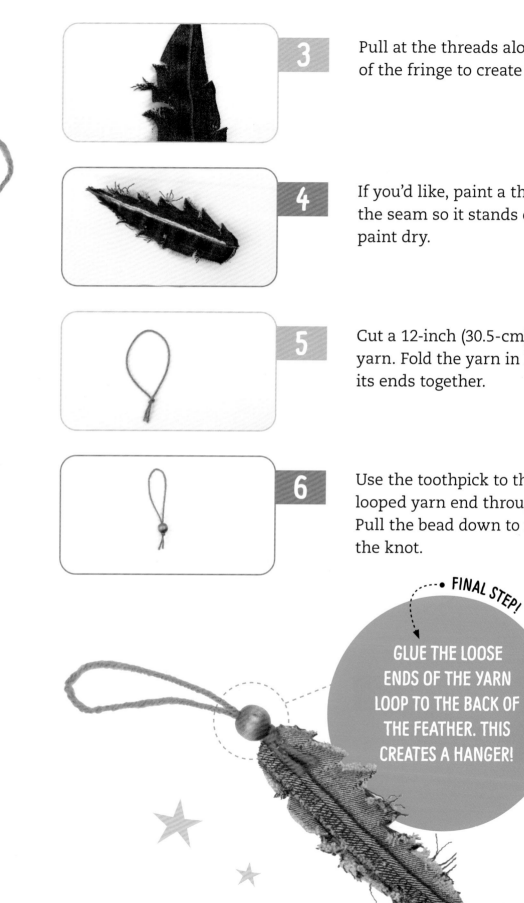

3 Pull at the threads along the edges of the fringe to create a frayed look.

4 If you'd like, paint a thin line along the seam so it stands out. Let the paint dry.

5 Cut a 12-inch (30.5-cm) length of yarn. Fold the yarn in half and knot its ends together.

6 Use the toothpick to thread the looped yarn end through the bead. Pull the bead down to rest on top of the knot.

• FINAL STEP!

GLUE THE LOOSE ENDS OF THE YARN LOOP TO THE BACK OF THE FEATHER. THIS CREATES A HANGER!

FISHING CAT TOY

LOOKING FOR SOMETHING TO DO IN YOUR FREE TIME? GO FISHING! YOU CAN USE OLD SOCKS TO CREATE SOME FISH FOR YOU AND YOUR FAVORITE FELINE.

WHAT YOU NEED

- string
- metal washer
- old socks
- toothpick
- old T-shirt scraps
- permanent marker
- paint and paintbrush
- wooden dowel

1 Tie one end of a string about 2 feet (0.6 meters) long to a metal washer.

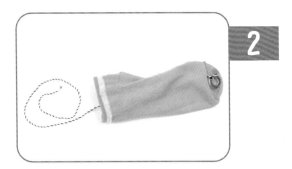

2 Turn a sock inside out. Use a toothpick to poke a small hole in the toe of the sock. Then thread the other end of the string through the hole until the washer is flush with the inside of the sock.

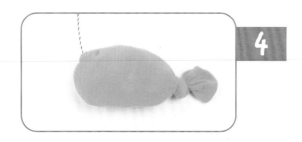

3 Turn the sock right side out. Stuff it with the T-shirt scraps. Leave the top few inches of the sock unstuffed.

4 Tie the top of the sock in a knot. This creates the fish's tail.

5 Use a marker to draw a face on the fish.

6 Repeat steps 1 through 5 to make as many fish as you'd like.

• FINAL STEP!

PAINT THE DOWEL AND LET IT DRY. THEN TIE THE END OF THE STRING TO ONE END OF THE DOWEL.

SCRUNCHIES

DO YOU HAVE OLD T-SHIRTS THAT ARE HARD TO PART WITH? DON'T THROW THEM OUT! INSTEAD, USE THOSE BELOVED SHIRTS TO MAKE SCRUNCHIES FOR YOU AND YOUR FRIENDS.

WHAT YOU NEED

- old T-shirt or tank top
- scissors
- ruler
- hot glue and hot glue gun
- 2 safety pins
- wide rubber or elastic band

1 Lay your shirt flat. Cut off the bottom seam. Then cut a strip off the bottom of the shirt that is 4.5 inches (11 cm) wide.

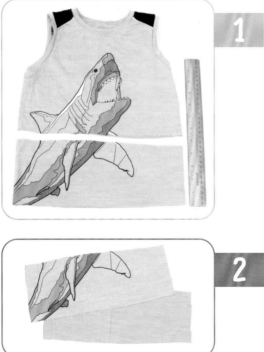

2 Cut the side seams off the strip. You will now have two rectangular pieces. Set one aside.

3 Fold a short end of the other rectangle in ½ inch (1.3 cm). Glue it in place to make a finished end.

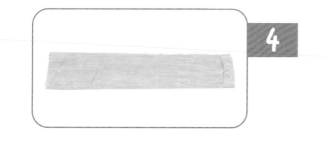

4 Flip the fabric over so the glued seam faces down. Now fold the full piece of fabric in half lengthwise so you can see the seam again. Glue the long, open edges of the fabric together. This creates a tube.

5 Have an adult help you attach a safety pin to the finished end you made in step 3.

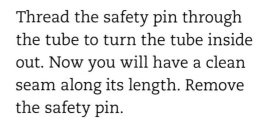

6 Thread the safety pin through the tube to turn the tube inside out. Now you will have a clean seam along its length. Remove the safety pin.

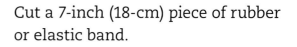

7 Cut a 7-inch (18-cm) piece of rubber or elastic band.

8 Have an adult help you attach a safety pin to each end of the band.

Project continued on the next page ▶

9 Thread the band through the fabric tube.

10 Remove the safety pins but continue to hold onto the ends of the band. Tie the band ends together in a tight knot.

11 Tuck the unfinished end of the fabric tube inside the finished end and glue it in place.

FINAL STEP!

USE THE PIECE YOU SET ASIDE IN STEP 3 TO MAKE ANOTHER SCRUNCHIE FOR A FRIEND!

LAUNDRY MONSTER

DO YOU EVER GET IN TROUBLE FOR LEAVING YOUR DIRTY CLOTHES ON THE FLOOR? TURN AN OLD TOWEL INTO A FUN LAUNDRY HOLDER THAT WILL GOBBLE ALL YOUR CLOTHES OFF THE FLOOR!

WHAT YOU NEED

- large bath towel
- safety pins
- ruler
- marker
- scissors
- hot glue and hot glue gun
- 2 buttons
- needle and thread
- felt

1 Lay the towel so its long edges are vertical on a flat surface. Fold up the bottom of the towel so it rests about 8 inches (20 cm) from the towel's top edge.

2 Ask an adult to help you close up the sides with safety pins. Secure the pin clasps on the back of the towel so they don't show on its front.

Project continued on the next page

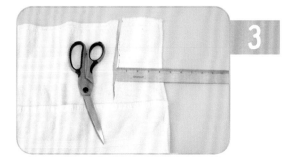

3 Along the top edge of the towel, measure 4 inches (10 cm) in from the right edge. Use the ruler and marker to draw a straight line from that point down to where the bottom edge of the towel rests. Do the same on the left side. Cut along the lines you drew.

4 Cut out the middle section at the top of the towel, leaving two flaps on either side. Glue together the edges of the towel running between the two side flaps.

5 Ask an adult to help you sew a button to the base of each flap.

6 Fold down the top of each flap to determine where it touches the button. Make small cuts in the flaps for the buttons to go through.

7 Button down the two flaps.

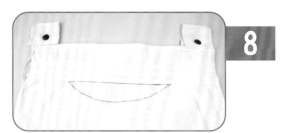

8 Draw the outline of a mouth near the top of the towel. The mouth should be at least 12 inches (30.5 cm) wide.

9 Cut the mouth out of the towel.

10 Cut out pieces of felt to create a mouth, eyes, and other features for your monster. Glue the felt to the towel. However, make sure you don't glue closed the bottom curve of the mouth—that is where the dirty laundry goes!

FINAL STEP!

UNDO THE BUTTONED FLAPS TO HANG YOUR LAUNDRY MONSTER ON A TOWEL RACK OR TWO TO THREE WALL HOOKS.

BRAIDED T-SHIRT BRACELET

YOUR FAVORITE SHIRT MAY BE WORN OR HAVE HOLES, BUT YOU CAN STILL WEAR IT—ON YOUR WRIST! TURN OLD TOPS INTO BRAIDED BRACELETS THAT YOU CAN WEAR FOR YEARS TO COME.

WHAT YOU NEED

- old T-shirt(s)
- scissors
- ruler
- marker
- tape
- hot glue and hot glue gun

1 Lay the T-shirt on a flat surface. Cut off the bottom hem and set it aside.

2 Cut a strip from the bottom of the shirt that is 1 ½ inches (4 cm) wide.

3 Cut the side seams off the strip from step 2. This will create two strips.

44

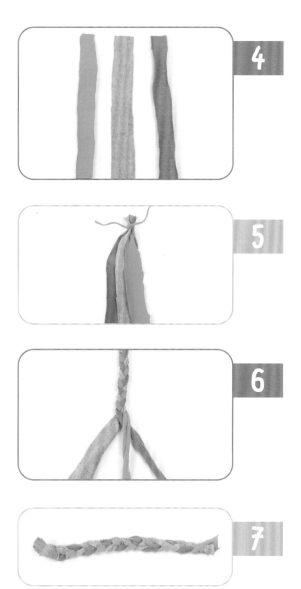

4 If your shirt is a solid color, repeat steps 1 through 3 with another shirt or two if you want your bracelet to be more than one color. Otherwise, repeat steps 2 and 3 with the same shirt. Either way, create at least three strips.

5 Choose three of the strips you've cut. Tie them together at one end using a thin strip of fabric cut from one of the shirts.

6 Tape the knotted end to a stable surface and begin braiding. Make the braid long enough to wrap around your wrist.

7 Once the braid is long enough, tie off the end with another piece of a cut shirt hem. Trim any extra length that is not braided.

FINAL STEP!

WRAP A PIECE OF CUT SHIRT HEM AROUND BOTH KNOTTED ENDS AND GLUE IN PLACE.

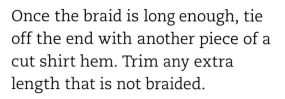

DOOR DRAFT BLOCKER

IS IT CHILLY OUTSIDE? KEEP COLD AIR FROM SNEAKING IN UNDER YOUR DOOR WITH THIS DRAFT BLOCKER MADE FROM AN OLD PILLOWCASE!

WHAT YOU NEED

- old pillowcase
- ruler
- marker
- scissors
- hot glue and hot glue gun
- old clothes or socks

1 Lay the pillowcase on a flat surface with the opening at the top.

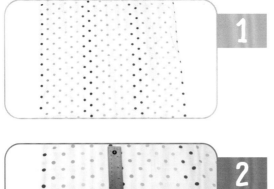

2 Measure 6 inches (15 cm) in from the bottom left corner. Use a ruler to draw a vertical line at this mark from the bottom to the top of the pillowcase.

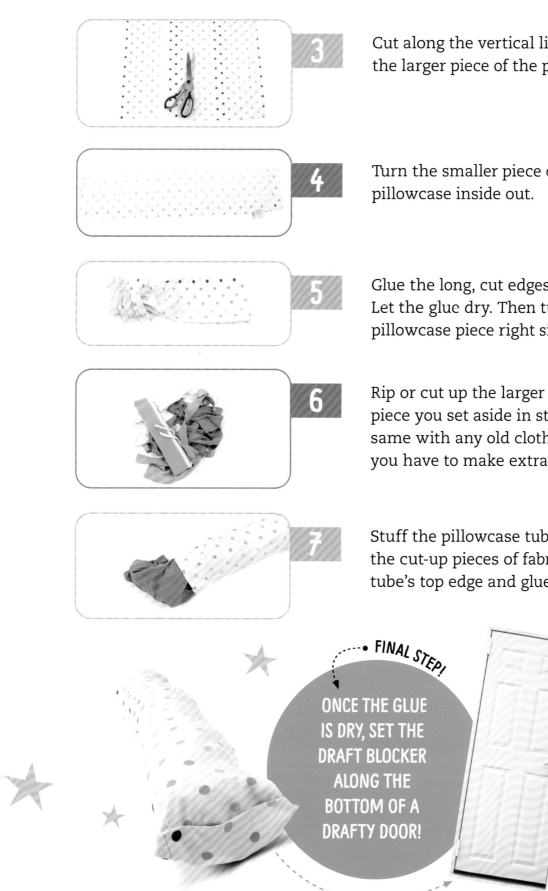

3 Cut along the vertical line. Set aside the larger piece of the pillowcase.

4 Turn the smaller piece of the pillowcase inside out.

5 Glue the long, cut edges together. Let the glue dry. Then turn the pillowcase piece right side out.

6 Rip or cut up the larger pillowcase piece you set aside in step 3. Do the same with any old clothes or socks you have to make extra filling.

7 Stuff the pillowcase tube full with the cut-up pieces of fabric. Fold the tube's top edge and glue it shut.

• FINAL STEP!

ONCE THE GLUE IS DRY, SET THE DRAFT BLOCKER ALONG THE BOTTOM OF A DRAFTY DOOR!

HANDY HAND WARMERS

DON'T LET THE COLD KEEP YOU INDOORS! POP THESE HAND WARMERS INTO YOUR MITTENS OR POCKETS TO KEEP YOUR FINGERS TOASTY!

WHAT YOU NEED

- old shirt
- lid with 6-inch (15-cm) diameter or cardboard and compass
- marker
- scissors
- uncooked rice
- microwave

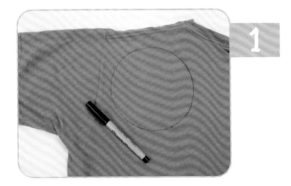

1 Lay the shirt flat on a surface. If you have a lid that is 6 inches (15 cm) in diameter, trace it on the shirt. If you don't have a lid, use a compass to draw that size circle on cardboard. Have an adult cut out the circle. Trace the circle on the shirt.

2 Cut out the traced circle. Make sure to cut through both layers of the shirt.

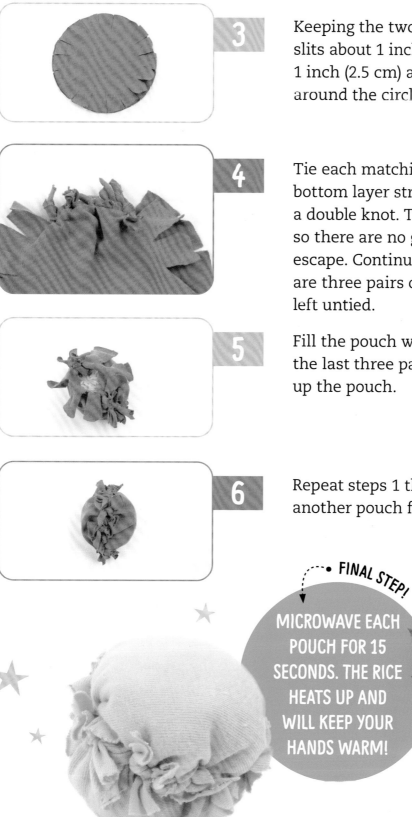

3 Keeping the two layers together, cut slits about 1 inch (2.5 cm) long and 1 inch (2.5 cm) apart all the way around the circles' edges.

4 Tie each matching top layer and bottom layer strip together with a double knot. Tie the knots tightly so there are no gaps for rice to escape. Continue until there are three pairs of strips in a row left untied.

5 Fill the pouch with rice. Then knot the last three pairs of strips to close up the pouch.

6 Repeat steps 1 through 5 to make another pouch for your other hand.

• FINAL STEP!

MICROWAVE EACH POUCH FOR 15 SECONDS. THE RICE HEATS UP AND WILL KEEP YOUR HANDS WARM!

FLANNEL SHIRT THROW PILLOW

FLANNEL IS A CLASSIC COMFORT. TURN AN OLD, SOFT FLANNEL SHIRT INTO A **PILLOW COVER** TO ADD A COZY TOUCH TO ANY ROOM!

WHAT YOU NEED

- large flannel shirt
- throw pillow
- ruler
- scissors
- hot glue and hot glue gun

1 Lay the flannel shirt on a flat surface. Make sure the shirt is buttoned.

2 Place the pillow on top of the body of the shirt.

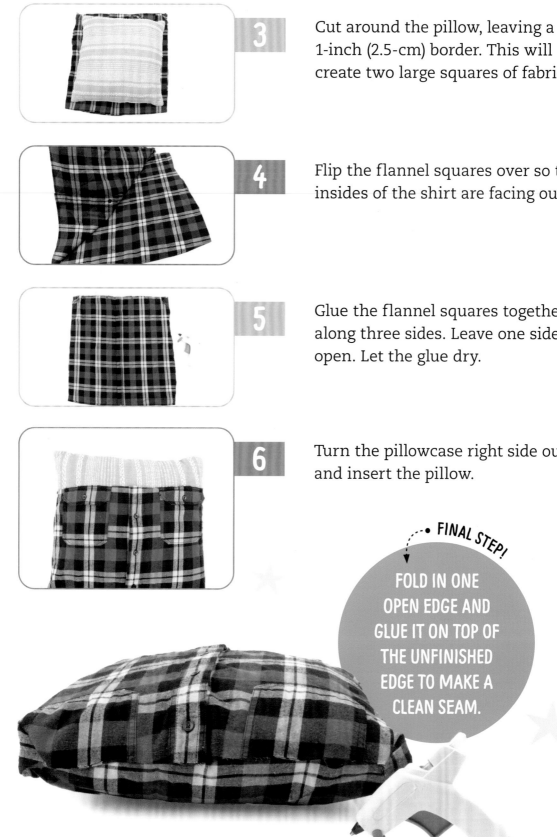

3 Cut around the pillow, leaving a 1-inch (2.5-cm) border. This will create two large squares of fabric.

4 Flip the flannel squares over so the insides of the shirt are facing out.

5 Glue the flannel squares together along three sides. Leave one side open. Let the glue dry.

6 Turn the pillowcase right side out and insert the pillow.

• FINAL STEP!

FOLD IN ONE OPEN EDGE AND GLUE IT ON TOP OF THE UNFINISHED EDGE TO MAKE A CLEAN SEAM.

SWEATER BEANIE

DO YOU HAVE A SWEATER THAT NO LONGER FITS YOU? TURN IT INTO A HAT! KEEP COZY WITH THIS HOMEMADE BEANIE.

WHAT YOU NEED

- old sweater
- ruler
- marker
- scissors
- winter hat
- hot glue and hot glue gun
- large pom-pom

1 Turn the sweater inside out and lay it flat on your work surface.

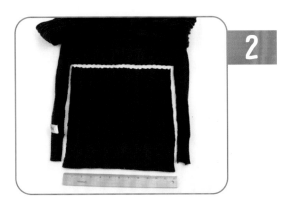

2 Draw a 12-inch (30.5-cm) square on the sweater. Use its bottom hem as the square's bottom edge. Cut out the square through both layers of the sweater.

3 Trim the sides and top corners of the square to make a hat shape. To be sure the beanie fits your head, trace one of your winter hats onto it before trimming the sides.

4 Glue the side and top edges of the two sweater layers together. Let the glue dry.

5 Turn your hat right side out and try it on!

FINAL STEP!

GLUE A LARGE POM-POM ATOP YOUR BEANIE TO ADD FLAIR!

PET BED

DO YOU HAVE A FURRY FRIEND? MAKE YOUR BUDDY A SOFT BED USING A WELL-WORN SWEATSHIRT!

WHAT YOU NEED

- old sweatshirt
- hot glue and hot glue gun
- marker
- old clothing (or plastic bags and newspapers)
- pillow (optional)
- scissors
- sock
- safety pins

1 Lay the sweatshirt on a flat surface. Glue the neck hole shut.

2 Draw a line from the bottom left armpit to the bottom right armpit. Make the line curve slightly upward.

3 On the inside of the sweatshirt, place a line of glue beneath the line you drew in step 2. Glue the front and back of the sweatshirt together along this line. This will seal off the bottom of the sweatshirt from the arms and upper chest.

4 Stuff the arms with old clothing. If you run out of clothing, use plastic bags and newspapers.

5 Keep stuffing until both arms and the chest area of the sweatshirt are plump and full.

6 Insert a pillow or more old clothing into the bottom of the sweatshirt.

Project continued on the next page ▶

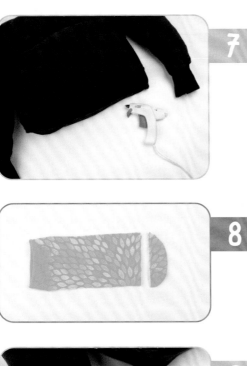

7 Glue the bottom hem of the sweatshirt shut.

8 Cut off the toe end of the sock to make a tube.

9 Slide the tube onto one of the sleeves.

10 With an adult's help, safety pin the ends of the sleeves together.

• FINAL STEP!

SLIDE THE SOCK TUBE OVER THE PINNED AREA TO CREATE A FINISHED LOOK.

ECO FACTS

Some clothing brands collect old clothes from customers and donate, resell, or repurpose the fabric. For example, Levi's recycles old denim into insulation for buildings!

RECYCLED PAPER PROJECTS

PAPER IS EVERYWHERE!

Loads of everyday items are made of paper, from calendars and magazines to gift bags and cardboard. When we're done using paper products, we usually toss them into the recycling bin. But why not use these materials to create fun, new, and useful items?

NOW, PULL OUT YOUR RECYCLING BIN, GRAB SOME PAINT AND GLUE, AND GET READY TO CRAFT!

WITH PAPER, THERE'S NO LIMIT TO WHAT YOU CAN CREATE.

SCRAP PAPER BOOKMARKS

WHAT DO YOU DO WITH OLD CALENDARS, MAGAZINES, AND GREETING CARDS? TURN THESE SCRAP PAPER ITEMS INTO **ARTISTIC BOOKMARKS!**

WHAT YOU NEED

- paperboard (cereal or cracker boxes)
- ruler
- scissors
- hole punch
- old magazines, calendars, or greeting cards
- glue stick
- yarn

1 Cut along the seams of the paperboard box to make a flat sheet. Measure a rectangle on the sheet that is 1½ by 6 inches (4 by 15 cm). Cut out the shape.

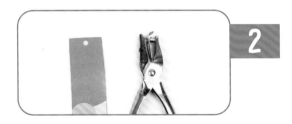

2 Use the hole punch to make a hole at one end of the rectangle.

3 Cut letters, words, and designs from the old magazines and other paper products.

4 Glue your cutouts to one side of the paperboard rectangle. Do not cover the hole.

5 Cut three 5-inch (13-cm) pieces of yarn.

6 Place the yarn pieces together then fold them in half to create a loop. Thread the loop end through the punched hole in the bookmark.

• FINAL STEP!

THREAD THE ENDS OF THE YARN THROUGH THE LOOP AND PULL TO TIGHTEN.

NEWSPAPER FLOWERS

DON'T DISCARD AN OLD NEWSPAPER! YOU CAN BRING A LITTLE SUNSHINE TO ANY SPACE WITH A BOUQUET OF PAPER FLOWERS.

WHAT YOU NEED

- newspaper (comics if you want color)
- ruler
- pencil
- scissors
- tape

1 Lay a sheet of newspaper on a flat work surface. Cut a 6-by-8-inch (15-by-20-cm) piece from the paper.

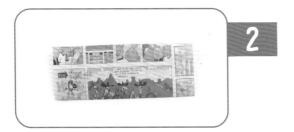

2 Fold the newspaper piece in half lengthwise. You will now have a 3-by-8-inch (8-by-20-cm) piece with two layers.

ECO FACTS

Japanese artist Chie Hitotsuyama uses strips of wet, rolled newspaper to create life-size animal sculptures. With newspaper, Hitotsuyama can imitate everything from fur to scales!

3 Place the paper piece so its folded edge is at the bottom. Then use a ruler to draw a horizontal line about ½ inch (1.3 cm) below the top edge.

4 Starting at the folded edge, cut the paper up to the line you made in step 3. Continue cutting slits that are about ⅛ inch (0.3 cm) apart across the length of the paper.

5 Wrap the uncut portion of the folded newspaper around a pencil top. Tape the paper to secure it.

FINAL STEP!

SPREAD OUT THE PETALS. THEN MAKE MORE FLOWERS TO FORM A BOUQUET!

MAP ENVELOPE

LOOK IN ANY GLOVE BOX AND YOU MAY FIND AN OLD PAPER MAP. TRANSFORM THAT MAP INTO AN ENVELOPE AND MAIL IT TO A FRIEND OR FAMILY MEMBER WHO LOVES TO TRAVEL!

GRANDPA BROWN
1640 RIVERSIDE DR.
HILL VALLEY, CA 95420

WHAT YOU NEED

- old map
- ruler
- pencil
- scissors
- tape
- paper
- marker
- address label (optional)
- postage

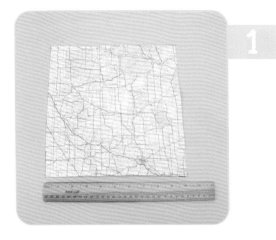

1 Ask permission from an adult before cutting up your chosen old map. Then open the map and lay it facedown on a flat surface. Measure and cut a square that is 10-by-10-inches (25-by-25-cm). Use the ruler and pencil to mark the center point along each side of the square. This will be at the 5-inch (12.5-cm) mark.

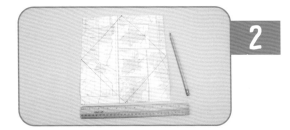

2 Draw four straight lines connecting the marks. This creates a center square.

3 Rotate the map so a corner is at the top. Fold its top corner in toward the center along one of the lines you made in step 2. Then fold in the bottom corner.

4 Rotate the map so its unfolded corners are at the top and bottom. Fold the bottom corner up so it overlaps slightly with the first two folded corners. Secure it with tape.

5 Place your letter inside the envelope and fold down the top corner. Use tape or a sticker to secure the flap. Then cut a shape from paper and tape it to the front of the envelope. Write the recipient's address in marker on the paper.

·····• FINAL STEP!

ADD A RETURN ADDRESS TO THE ENVELOPE AND HAVE AN ADULT HELP YOU FIGURE OUT HOW MUCH POSTAGE THE ENVELOPE NEEDS. SQUARE ENVELOPES COST MORE TO SEND.

MAGAZINE TUBE ANIMAL

ADD A SPLASH OF COLOR TO YOUR ROOM WITH SOME **3D ART**! GATHER OLD MAGAZINES AND GET STARTED ON YOUR VERY OWN MASTERPIECE.

WHAT YOU NEED

- scissors
- paperboard (cereal or cracker boxes)
- pencil
- magazines
- tape
- hot glue and hot glue gun
- paint and paintbrush

1 Cut along the paperboard box seams to remove one large, flat side. Draw an animal shape on the paperboard and cut it out.

2 Tear out several pages from the magazines. Roll each page into a tube and use tape to secure it.

ECO FACTS

Magazine paper often has a special coating that gives it a smooth, glossy finish. This paper can be recycled. But first, see if any local organizations, such as libraries or shelters, will take your used magazines for others to read!

3 Lay the tubes on top of your animal cutout. Use hot glue to attach the tubes to the paperboard. Let the glue dry.

4 After the glue has dried, cut the tubes along the outline of the paperboard animal.

•---• FINAL STEP!

USE HOT GLUE TO MOUNT YOUR ANIMAL TO A SQUARE OF PAINTED CARDBOARD. THEN DISPLAY IT!

PAPER BAG TREE HANGER

PLANT A **TREE** INDOORS! A PAPER GROCERY BAG BECOMES A BRANCHED HANGER FOR EARRINGS, EAR BUDS, BRACELETS, AND MORE.

WHAT YOU NEED

- paper grocery bag or packing paper
- ruler
- scissors
- wire and wire cutter
- clear tape
- hot glue and hot glue gun
- paint and paintbrush

1 Cut the paper bag along one side and its bottom seams, and then lay it out flat. Then cut the bag into strips that are about 2 inches (5 cm) wide.

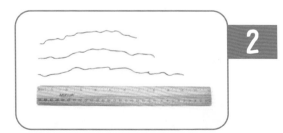

2 Ask an adult to help you cut three wire pieces of varying lengths. Make each piece between 6 and 10 inches (15 and 25 cm) long.

3

Tightly wrap a strip of paper bag around one of the wires, covering it from end to end. Tape the paper strip to secure it. Repeat with the other two pieces of wire and paper strips to make three pieces total.

4

Have an adult help you cut an additional piece of wire. Wrap the wire around the pieces from step 4 to create a tree trunk. Leave the ends loose as branches and roots.

5

Wrap another paper strip around the trunk to cover the wire. Twist the strip as you go to create texture. Secure the paper with tape.

6

To make more branches, glue more paper strips to the trunk and then twist them.

•••► FINAL STEP!

BEND THE ROOTS SO THE TREE CAN STAND ON ITS OWN. PAINT YOUR TREE FOR EXTRA FLAIR!

MESSAGE BOARD

THE PAGES OF OLD BOOKS AND MAGAZINES CREATE THE PERFECT BACKDROP TO THIS HOMEMADE MESSAGE BOARD. ADD POPS OF COLOR WITH BITS OF USED WRAPPING PAPER!

WHAT YOU NEED

- corrugated cardboard
- utility knife
- hot glue and hot glue gun
- old magazine or book
- scissors
- decoupage glue
- foam brush
- used wrapping paper
- markers (optional)
- string
- duct tape
- pushpins

1 Decide how big you want your message board to be. Then ask an adult to help you cut three pieces of corrugated cardboard to that size. Stack the pieces and hot glue the layers together.

2 Cut out pages of text from an old magazine or book. Cut enough to cover one side of your message board.

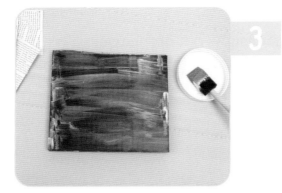

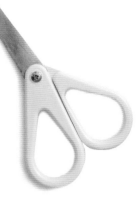

3 Brush a thin coat of decoupage glue on one side of the message board.

4 Lay the cut pages of text on the decoupage glue. Overlap them until the cardboard is covered. Trim any paper that extends beyond the cardboard's edges.

5 Add another thin coat of decoupage glue over the pages. Let them dry.

ECO FACTS

Nearly half of all corrugated boxes made in the United States each year are used to ship food from farms to grocery stores.

Project continued on the next page

6 Cut designs out of the used wrapping paper.

7 Glue your cut designs on top of the board using decoupage glue.

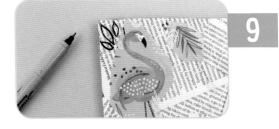

8 Cover the board with another thin coat of decoupage glue. Let it dry.

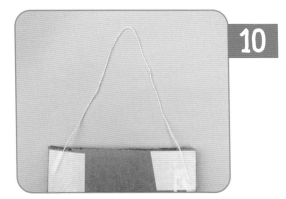

9 If you'd like, use markers to add any other details or designs to your board.

10 Cut a piece of string about 18 inches (46 cm) long. Tape the ends of the string to the back of the message board.

FINAL STEP!

HANG THE BOARD
UP BY THE STRING.
USE PUSHPINS TO
ATTACH MESSAGES
TO THE BOARD!

To Do :
☑ call Jamal
☑ card for Grandma
☑ clean room
☐ fix bike seat

Write
book report
!!!

TISSUE PAPER SUNCATCHER

SUNCATCHERS MAKE ANY SPACE CHEERFUL AND BRIGHT. MAKE A COLORFUL ONE OUT OF REPURPOSED TISSUE PAPER!

WHAT YOU NEED

- card stock
- pencil
- marker
- scissors
- clear contact paper
- tissue paper
- hole punch
- string

1 Draw a simple shape or object on a sheet of card stock. Use a marker to make the outline thick.

2 Cut out the paper inside the outline of your shape. Ask an adult for help if you need it.

74

3 Trim away the paper outside the outline as well. This will leave a cutout of the shape's outline.

4 Cut a piece of contact paper slightly larger than your cutout from step 3. Lay the contact paper on a flat work surface, sticky side up. Remove the backing. Carefully place your cutout on top of the contact paper.

5 Cut or tear pieces of tissue paper and stick them to the contact paper inside your cutout. Continue until the cutout is filled in.

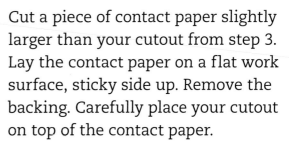

6 Carefully lay another piece of contact paper, sticky side down, over the top of your design. Then trim off all extra contact paper around your design.

7 Punch a hole into the top of your suncatcher.

··•· FINAL STEP!

TIE A STRING THROUGH THE HOLE AND HANG YOUR SUNCATCHER IN A WINDOW!

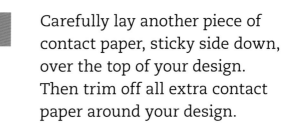

BROWN BAG JOURNAL

NEED SOMEWHERE TO PUT YOUR THOUGHTS? BIND YOUR OWN JOURNAL WITH A NEEDLE, THREAD, AND A BROWN GROCERY BAG!

WHAT YOU NEED

- 5 sheets of writing paper
- ruler
- scissors
- brown grocery bag
- pencil
- safety pin
- needle
- thread
- markers or other decorative materials

1 Cut the five sheets of paper in half across their width.

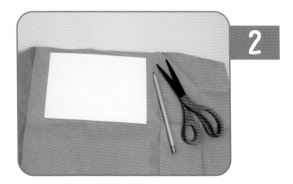

2 Cut open a brown grocery bag. Trace one of the half sheets onto the bag and cut out the shape. This will be the journal cover.

3 Stack the pieces of writing paper so the long edges are horizontal. Then fold the pieces in half vertically.

4 Fold the cover piece in half the same way you did the writing paper in step 3. Then slide the folded writing paper into the cover.

5 Open the journal to the center page. Measure and mark five evenly spaced dots along the crease of the journal.

6 With an adult's help, poke through the dots with a safety pin, making a hole through each layer of paper and the cover.

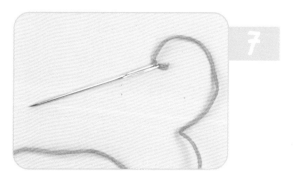

7 Measure and cut about 24 inches (61 cm) of thread. Thread one end through the eye of the needle and knot it onto the needle.

Project continued on the next page

8 With an adult's help, insert the needle through the middle hole inside the journal. Pull the thread through the hole until there is a tail of thread about 2 inches (5 cm) long.

9 From outside the journal, insert the needle through the hole above the one you just came through. Pull the thread through.

10 Insert the needle through the top hole from inside the journal.

11 Insert the needle through the previous hole from the outside then through the middle hole.

12 Repeat steps 9 to 11, but on the bottom end of the journal.

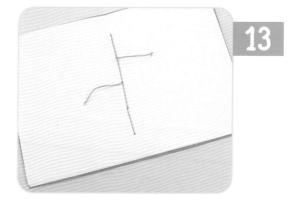

13 Push the needle through one more outside hole (above the middle) so the needle ends up back inside the journal. Cut the thread, leaving another 2-inch (5-cm) tail.

14 Knot the two tails together. Trim any extra thread.

FINAL STEP!

DECORATE YOUR JOURNAL'S COVER USING MARKERS, STICKERS, SCRAP PAPER, GLUE, AND MORE!

BUTTERFLY GARLAND

CRAFT COLORFUL BUTTERFLIES OUT OF MAGAZINE PAGES AND STRING THEM INTO A **UNIQUE GARLAND**. THESE FLUTTERING INSECTS WILL CREATE BEAUTY WHEREVER THEY HANG!

WHAT YOU NEED

- magazine pages
- ruler
- pencil
- scissors
- yarn

1 Cut a 6-inch (15-cm) square from a colorful magazine page.

2 Fold the square in half, corner to corner, to form a triangle. Fold so the colorful imagery is on the outside of the triangle.

3 Accordion fold the triangle.

4 Pinching the middle of the accordioned piece, fold the two ends upward, so the piece makes a V shape. This creates one top set of butterfly wings.

5 Cut a 4-inch (10-cm) square from another colorful magazine page.

6 Repeat steps 2 through 4 to create a smaller bottom wing set.

Project continued on the next page

7 Lay the wing sets together with their center folds touching. The larger set should be on top. Cut and knot a piece of yarn around the meeting point. Cut off any extra length.

8 Carefully fan out the wings to make them larger.

9 Repeat steps 1 through 8 to make more butterflies.

ECO FACTS

Recycling organizations turn old magazines into many new paper products. These include paperboard, printer paper, and tissue paper.

10 Cut a piece of yarn as long as you'd like your garland to be. Tie one end of the yarn around the center of the first butterfly. Leave about 6 inches (15 cm) of extra yarn at the top of the garland.

• FINAL STEP!

TIE BUTTERFLIES DOWN THE LENGTH OF THE YARN. THEN HANG YOUR GARLAND OF BEAUTIFUL BUGS!

GIFT BAG ORNAMENT

DO YOU HAVE A PILE OF USED GIFT BAGS STASHED AWAY FROM PAST PARTIES? USE THEM TO MAKE FESTIVE ORNAMENTS FOR YOUR NEXT CELEBRATION!

WHAT YOU NEED

- large, used gift bag
- scissors
- ruler
- pencil
- hole punch
- wire and wire cutter
- pliers
- decorative beads
- hot glue and hot glue gun
- string

1 Cut the gift bag down one side and along the base so it can lie flat.

2 Cut 12 strips from the gift bag, each 10 by 1 inch (25 by 2.5 cm). Then punch three holes in each strip: one at each end and one in the middle.

ECO FACTS

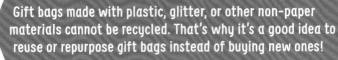

Gift bags made with plastic, glitter, or other non-paper materials cannot be recycled. That's why it's a good idea to reuse or repurpose gift bags instead of buying new ones!

3

Ask an adult to help you cut an 8-inch (20-cm) piece of wire. Then have the adult use pliers to make a small loop at one end of the wire.

4

Thread a decorative bead onto the wire so it rests on the loop.

5

Thread each paper strip onto the wire through its middle hole. The colored side of the paper strips should face the decorative bead. Fan out the strips.

6

Take the ends of the topmost strip and thread them onto the wire. Glue the ends of the strip together. Repeat with each strip until all have been threaded onto the wire and glued.

7

Thread another decorative bead onto the wire. Ask an adult to loop the wire to keep the bead in place. Cut off any extra wire.

• FINAL STEP!

CUT A PIECE OF STRING AND THREAD IT THROUGH ONE OF THE WIRE LOOPS. KNOT THE STRING INTO A HANGER!

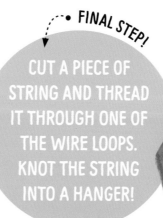

UPCYCLED PLASTIC PROJECTS

THERE'S
NO LIMIT TO
WHAT YOU CAN
CREATE WITH
PLASTIC!

NOW, GRAB SOME
PLASTICS IN YOUR
RECYCLING BIN, AND
GET READY TO CRAFT!

PLASTIC IS EVERYWHERE!

Loads of everyday items are made of plastic, from milk cartons and juice bottles to shopping bags and food containers. When we're done using plastic products, we usually toss them into the recycling bin. But why not use these materials to create fun, new, and useful items?

LUCKY CHARM

EVERYONE WOULD LOVE A LITTLE EXTRA LUCK IN THEIR LIVES. THESE CHARMS MAKE PERFECT GIFTS FOR FRIENDS AND FAMILY!

WHAT YOU NEED

- clear plastic container
- ruler
- scissors
- bottle cap
- green permanent marker
- pushpin
- toothpick
- dimensional glue
- jump ring
- bracelet

1 Cut a square from the plastic container that is 1½ by 1½ inches (4 by 4 cm). Use the marker to trace the bottle cap on the square. Then cut out the circle.

2 Draw a four-leaf clover on the circle of plastic.

ECO FACTS

A Netherlands-based company makes jewelry out of gold and silver from recycled mobile phones. The company's name, Nowa, stands for "No Waste."

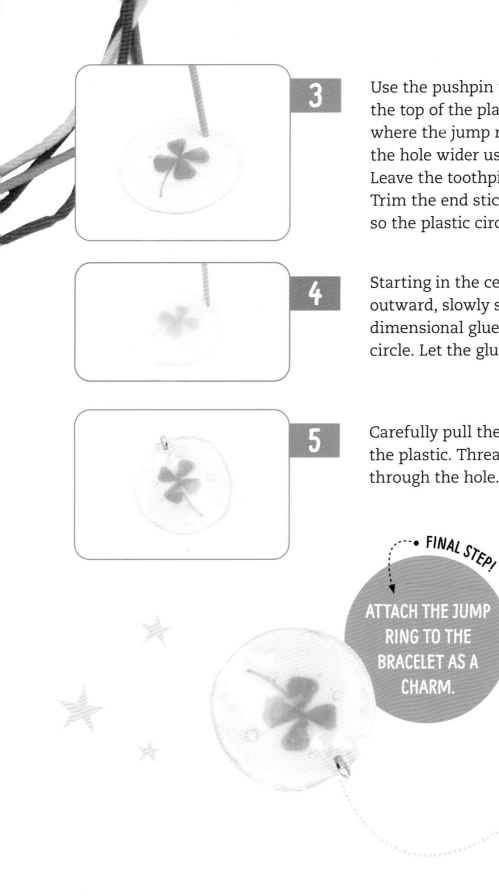

3 Use the pushpin to poke a hole near the top of the plastic circle. This is where the jump ring will go. Make the hole wider using the toothpick. Leave the toothpick in the hole. Trim the end sticking out the back so the plastic circle lies flat.

4 Starting in the center and working outward, slowly squeeze a layer of dimensional glue over the plastic circle. Let the glue dry.

5 Carefully pull the toothpick out of the plastic. Thread the jump ring through the hole.

FINAL STEP!

ATTACH THE JUMP RING TO THE BRACELET AS A CHARM.

PINWHEEL

DO YOU HAVE AN OUTDOOR SPACE THAT COULD USE SOME COLOR? THIS CHEERY PINWHEEL IS A FUN ADDITION TO A GARDEN OR POTTED PLANT.

WHAT YOU NEED

- plastic milk jug
- ruler
- scissors
- permanent markers
- pushpin
- toothpick
- brad
- dowel

1 Ask an adult to help you cut a 4-inch (10-cm) square from the plastic jug.

2 Decorate the plastic square with markers.

ECO FACTS

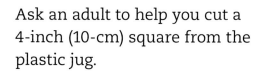

American toy company Green Toys makes all of its products out of recycled plastic. The main ingredient in these products is recycled milk jugs!

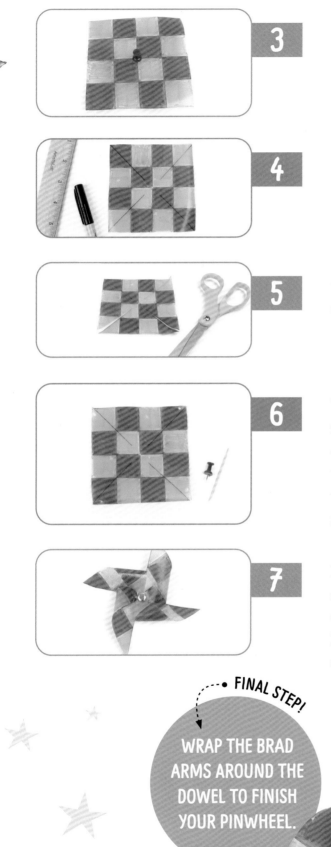

3 Use a ruler to find the center of the square. Make a small hole there using the pushpin. Use the toothpick to widen the hole.

4 Draw a straight line from each corner toward the center hole. Stop each line ½ inch (1.3 cm) from the hole.

5 Cut along the lines you made in step 4.

6 Use the pushpin and toothpick to make a hole in the right corner of each section of the pinwheel. Rotate the pinwheel clockwise as you work to help keep track of which is the right corner.

7 Bend each right corner so its hole overlaps the center hole. Do not crease the flaps as you bend them. Push a brad through all the holes and hold it in place.

FINAL STEP!

WRAP THE BRAD ARMS AROUND THE DOWEL TO FINISH YOUR PINWHEEL.

ANIMAL DECOR

DO YOU HAVE PLASTIC TOYS LYING AROUND THAT YOU NO LONGER PLAY WITH? DON'T THROW THEM OUT! A LITTLE PAINT CAN TURN THESE TOYS INTO STYLISH DECOR!

WHAT YOU NEED

- small plastic toys, such as animals
- paint and paintbrush
- hot glue and hot glue gun
- decor items such as a clothespin, jar with lid, and/or plastic lid

1 Decide which plastic toys to use. Then choose the decor items the toys will fit on top of or that can be attached to the toys.

2 Choose where you want to display your creations. Paint the toys colors to match the surrounding decor.

3 To make a message holder, glue a painted clothespin to the back of a toy.

4 To stylize a jar, paint its lid and glue a painted toy on top.

5 To make a trinket tray, paint a plastic lid. Then glue a painted toy inside it.

GOOD DAY

• FINAL STEP!

ONCE THE GLUE DRIES, PUT YOUR DECOR TO USE!

PENCIL HOLDER

PLASTIC BAGS NOT ONLY CLUTTER UP OUR HOMES, THEY CLUTTER UP OUR EARTH. KEEP PLASTIC BAGS OUT OF OCEANS AND LANDFILLS BY TURNING THEM INTO A COOL PENCIL HOLDER!

WHAT YOU NEED

- 12 plastic shopping bags
- scissors
- ruler
- tape
- recycled plastic container (tall enough to hold pencils)
- hot glue and hot glue gun

1 Lay a plastic bag flat on a hard work surface. Cut off the handles and the bottom of the bag.

2 Cut down one side of the bag. You should still have one side of the bag folded and connected. Rotate your bag so this side is at the top.

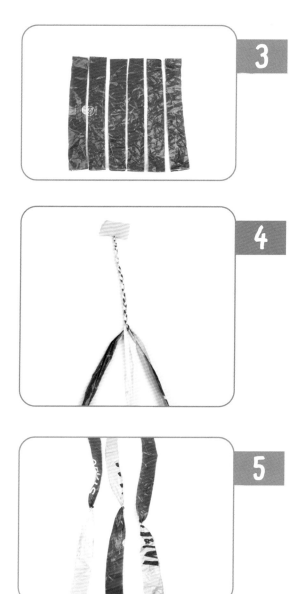

3 Cut the bag into vertical strips that are about 2 inches (5 cm) wide. Cut the other bags into strips the same way. Then unfold all strips.

4 Cut a small strip of plastic from the cut off bag handles and use it to tie three strips together at one end. Use tape to secure this end to a surface. Then braid the strips. If you want the braid to be thicker, use six strips and double them up before braiding.

5 As you near the bottom of the braid, tie another strip onto each existing one to add more length. Then continue braiding.

ECO FACTS — U.S. shoppers use an average of one plastic bag per day.

Project continued on the next page

6 Continue adding and braiding more strips. Work until the braided strip is between 8 and 12 feet (2.4 to 3.6 meters) long.

7 Knot the end of your braid. Use hot glue to attach the finished braid along the bottom edge of the container.

8 Continue wrapping the braid around the entire container, gluing the braid to it every few inches.

• FINAL STEP!

IF YOU RUN OUT OF BRAID
BEFORE YOU GET TO THE
TOP OF THE CONTAINER,
MAKE ANOTHER BRAID
AND CONTINUE GLUING
WHERE YOU LEFT OFF.
TRIM ANY EXTRA BRAID.

TROLL HOME

ARE TROLLS REAL? WE MAY NEVER KNOW. BUT WHY NOT BUILD A COZY TROLL HOME JUST IN CASE? THIS COLORFUL PLASTIC BOTTLE HUT IS A SWEET OFFERING TO ANY MYTHICAL CREATURE!

WHAT YOU NEED

- small soda bottle
- craft or utility knife
- scissors
- ruler
- paint and paintbrush
- glue
- acorns, sticks, and other natural materials
- LED candle

1 Ask an adult to cut off the top third of the bottle. Set it aside.

2 Have an adult help you trim about 2 inches (5 cm) off the remaining bottle. Recycle the piece you cut off.

ECO FACTS

Nearly 1 million plastic drink bottles are sold every minute in the world.

98

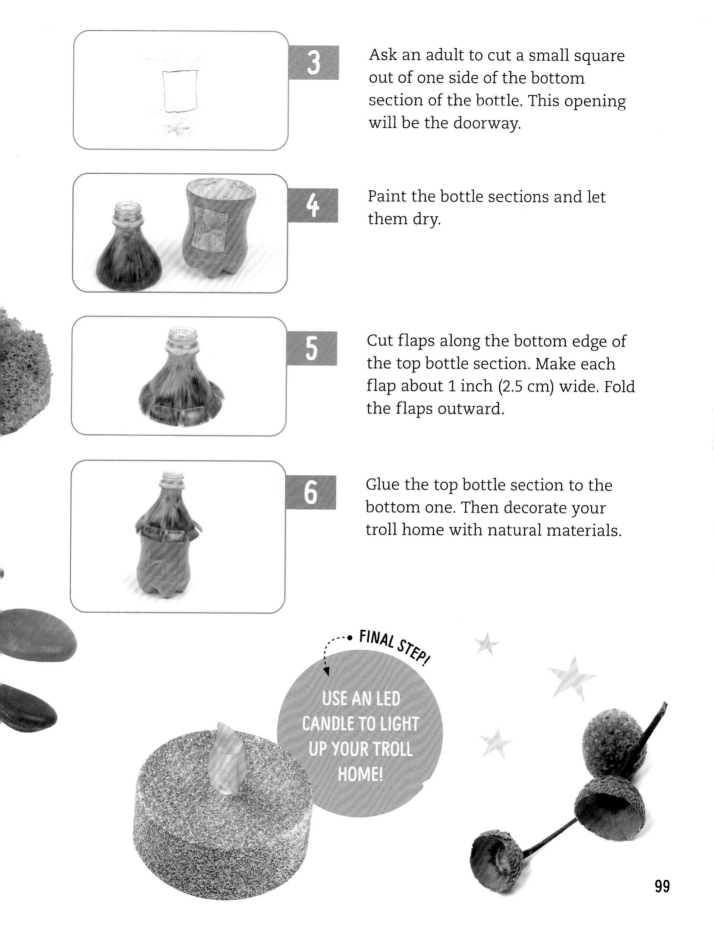

3 Ask an adult to cut a small square out of one side of the bottom section of the bottle. This opening will be the doorway.

4 Paint the bottle sections and let them dry.

5 Cut flaps along the bottom edge of the top bottle section. Make each flap about 1 inch (2.5 cm) wide. Fold the flaps outward.

6 Glue the top bottle section to the bottom one. Then decorate your troll home with natural materials.

• FINAL STEP!

USE AN LED CANDLE TO LIGHT UP YOUR TROLL HOME!

BIRD FEEDER

THE SOUND OF BIRDS CHIRPING IS A SURE SIGN OF SPRING. REUSE AN OLD PLASTIC TAKEOUT CONTAINER TO GIVE YOUR BACKYARD VISITORS A PLACE TO **PERCH AND EAT!**

WHAT YOU NEED

- rectangular plastic container with lid
- paint and paintbrush
- pushpin
- pencil
- twine
- ruler
- scissors
- birdseed

1 Wash and dry the plastic container and lid.

2 Paint the container and lid in a pattern inspired by nature. This could be a birch bark design, wood grain, leaf pattern, or others. Let the paint dry.

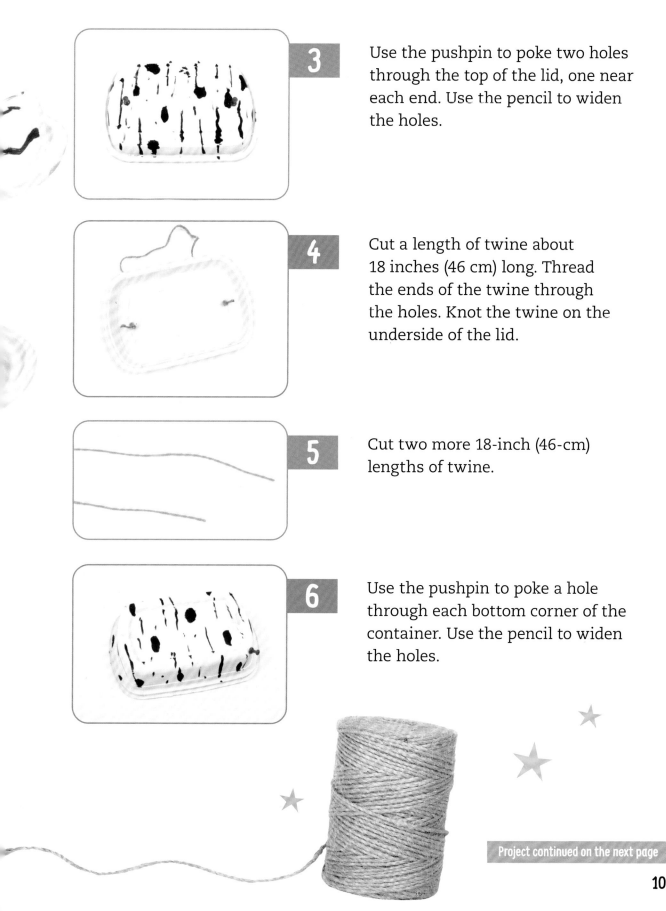

3 Use the pushpin to poke two holes through the top of the lid, one near each end. Use the pencil to widen the holes.

4 Cut a length of twine about 18 inches (46 cm) long. Thread the ends of the twine through the holes. Knot the twine on the underside of the lid.

5 Cut two more 18-inch (46-cm) lengths of twine.

6 Use the pushpin to poke a hole through each bottom corner of the container. Use the pencil to widen the holes.

Project continued on the next page

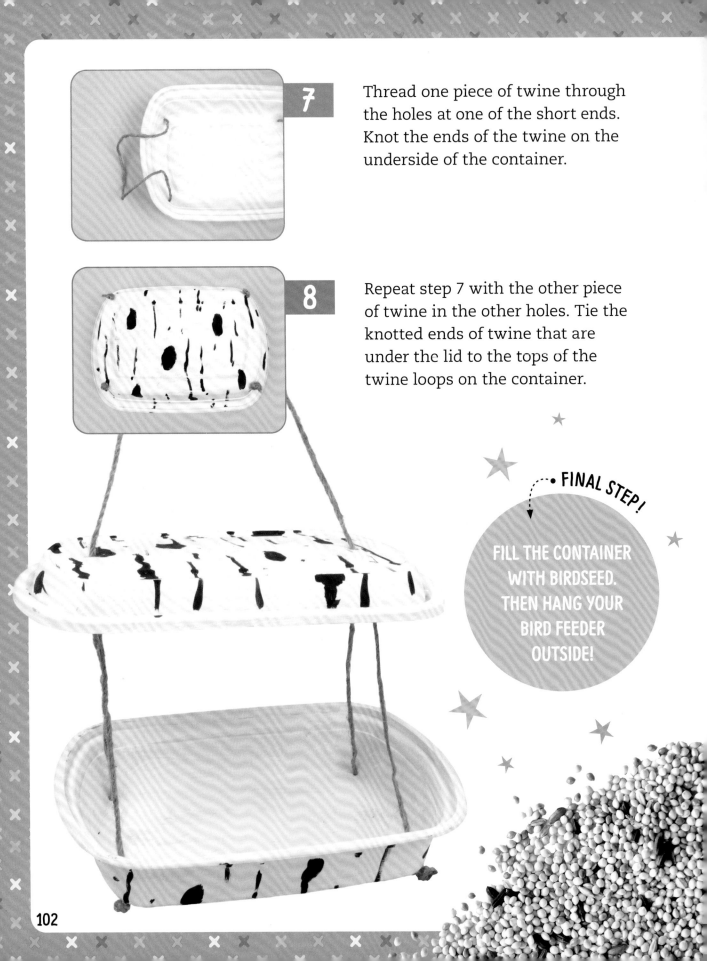

7 Thread one piece of twine through the holes at one of the short ends. Knot the ends of the twine on the underside of the container.

8 Repeat step 7 with the other piece of twine in the other holes. Tie the knotted ends of twine that are under the lid to the tops of the twine loops on the container.

• FINAL STEP!

FILL THE CONTAINER WITH BIRDSEED. THEN HANG YOUR BIRD FEEDER OUTSIDE!

OUTDOOR PILLOW

SITTING ON THE GROUND CAN GET UNCOMFORTABLE. A CUSHION CAN MAKE IT SOFTER! USE UP OLD PLASTIC SHOPPING BAGS TO MAKE YOURSELF A WEATHERPROOF PILLOW.

WHAT YOU NEED

- ruler
- several colors of duct tape
- scissors
- 25 plastic grocery bags

1 Decide how large you want your pillow to be. Cut a strip of duct tape the length of your pillow. Lay the strip sticky side up on a flat surface.

2 Cut another strip of duct tape the same length. The second strip should overlap the first by ¼ inch (0.6 cm).

Project continued on the next page >

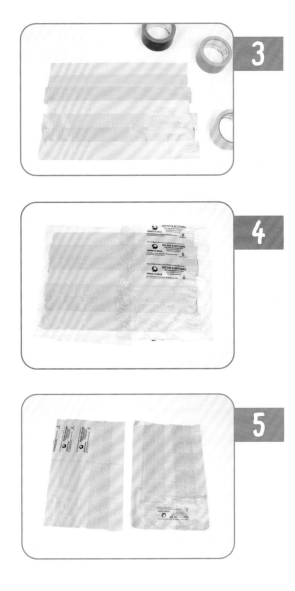

3 Continue laying down overlapping duct tape strips until you reach your desired pillow height.

4 Cut open a plastic shopping bag and lay it flat over the sticky duct tape strips. Trim any excess plastic bag.

5 Repeat the process to create a second piece of duct tape strips covered in plastic. Make this piece the same dimensions as the first piece.

6 Lay the two pieces on top of each other with their plastic sides facing out. Tape the pieces together along three sides.

ECO FACTS

In 2019, sportswear company Adidas unveiled its development of a line of fully recyclable shoes called FUTURECRAFT.LOOP. After a user wears out a pair of these shoes, Adidas breaks it down to recycle parts of it into a new pair!

7 Turn the pillow right side out. The colored sides of the duct tape should be facing out.

8 Stuff the pillow with plastic shopping bags.

•-- FINAL STEP!

WHEN YOUR PILLOW IS FILLED, USE ANOTHER STRIP OF DUCT TAPE TO CLOSE UP ITS OPEN SIDE.

BOTTLE CAP TIC-TAC-TOE

STUCK INDOORS ON A RAINY DAY? TIRED OF WATCHING TV? THIS MINI **BOARD GAME** IS PERFECT FOR DOWNTIME ENTERTAINMENT.

WHAT YOU NEED

- 10 plastic bottle caps
- paint and paintbrush
- cardboard
- ruler
- utility knife or scissors
- duct tape
- permanent marker (optional)

1 Paint the bottle caps and let them dry.

2 Ask an adult to help you cut an 8-by-8-inch (20-by-20-cm) square of cardboard.

3 Cover the cardboard square in colorful duct tape.

4 Use marker or strips of another color of duct tape to create two vertical lines and two horizontal lines on the square. This makes a tic-tac-toe board.

FINAL STEP!

USE PAINT OR A MARKER TO DRAW AN 'X' ON FIVE BOTTLE CAPS AND AN 'O' ON FIVE OTHERS. LET THE CAPS DRY. YOU'RE READY TO PLAY!

BEWARE: DINO!

DO YOU HAVE A GARDEN OR YARD THAT NEEDS PROTECTION? CREATE A FEARSOME DINOSAUR GUARD TO SCARE AWAY ANY PEST THAT COMES SNIFFING AROUND!

WHAT YOU NEED

- 2 empty juice bottles (1 for the dino head, 1 for the dino body
- paint and paintbrush
- scissors
- empty white plastic container (for teeth, eyes, feet, arms, and tail)
- hot glue and hot glue gun
- black permanent marker

1 Rinse and dry the plastic bottles and peel off any labels.

2 Paint the bottles and let them dry.

ECO FACTS

Globally, only about 9 percent of plastic waste is recycled.

3 Have an adult help you cut teeth out of the white plastic container. Glue them to the bottom of the bottle that you plan to use for the head.

4 Ask an adult to help you cut eyes out of the plastic container. Use the marker to draw pupils. Then glue the eyes onto the head. Glue on plastic eyebrows too if you'd like.

5 Turn the head upside down. Place the opening of the other bottle on the bottom of the head. Trace around the opening.

6 Have an adult cut out the circle you traced.

7 Push the top of the body bottle into the hole you made in step 6. Seal the connection with glue.

FINAL STEP!

CUT OUT AND PAINT MORE PLASTIC PIECES TO MAKE FEET, ARMS, AND A TAIL. GLUE THEM TO THE BODY.

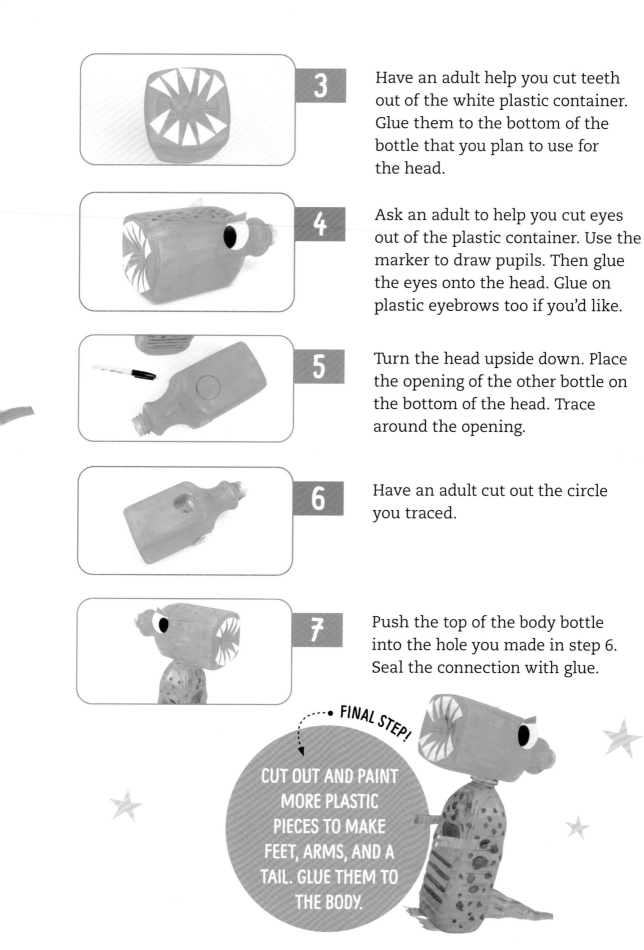

WATERPROOF GADGETS BAG

PLASTIC SANDWICH BAGS DON'T HAVE TO BE USED JUST ONCE! STYLE ONE WITH TAPE TO MAKE A WATERPROOF BAG THAT WILL KEEP YOUR ELECTRONICS SAFE.

WHAT YOU NEED

- lightly used sealable sandwich bag
- duct tape or decorative tape
- scissors

1 Wash and dry the sandwich bag. Lay it flat on a surface.

2 Cut three strips of tape as long as the bag's width. Place one strip along the bag's top edge. Trim the tape along the edge of the bag. Place the second strip along the top of the bag on the other side. Trim the tape along the edge of the bag. Place the third strip along the bottom edge. Fold the tape over so it covers both sides of the bag's edge.

3 Cut two strips of tape as long as the bag's height. Place one strip along each side edge of the bag. Fold the tape over so the back edges of the bag are covered too.

4 Cut a design out of the pieces of tape. If the tape's stickiness makes doing this difficult, ask an adult for help. Stick the pieces to the front of the bag.

FINAL STEP!

PUT SMALL ELECTRONICS INTO THE BAG. THEN SEAL IT FOR SAFEKEEPING!